# Clyde Valley
## *in the olden days*
### Kenneth Liddell & Alex F. Young

Garrion Mill from the south.

A group of fruit pickers somewhere in the valley in the late 1920s. Fruit pickers were drafted into the valley every year, living in bothies or boarding houses, for the six or eight week season, and in 1913 were visited by a deputation from the Royal Housing Commission. It is not known where they were working, but from the box seating the old man in the centre, the produce was going to George Carruthers & Sons, fruit merchants (founded 1922) in Glasgow's Candleriggs Market.

The Clyde Valley has been in decline as a major fruit growing area for decades, and many acres of former orchard now lie neglected. However, the formation of the Clyde Valley Orchard Group is an attempt to catalogue and protect the remaining tracts of productive orchard, and to encourage new planting of traditional Clyde Valley orchard varieties of fruit, not as a viable business but to conserve the rich and fruity past of the area.

## Acknowledgements

Beth Anderson, Alan Brotchie, Andrew Claase, Pearl Murphy and David Young of Hamilton Town House Library, Robert Sommerville Fairley, Rita Fairley, Evelyn Grant, Mrs Margaret Hill, Elizabeth Jack, Mrs Kathe Johnstone of Crossford, James Naismith of Lucindabank, Harry Corbett, Christine Edge, James Forrest, Lynne Gourlay, Marie Gray, Mrs Jean Howitt, Keith S Mason of the Church of Scotland, Rev. Dr. D. Cameron McPherson of Dalserf, Bill Muir, Alex Muirhead, Sadie Newlands, Mrs J Pinkerton, David Roberts, Ronald and Esther Scott, Jim Shanks of Newtonhead Farm, Kilmaurs, Ronald Stodart, Rory Templeman of Scottish Water, Jim Turner, Andrew Wilson of the National Library of Scotland, the late Janet Murray, The late John Murray, Mrs Agnes Murray, Paul Archibald, Iain McIver, Janet Stewart, John Christison and Tom Hislop.

## Illustration Acknowledgements

Pages 60 lower, 61 lower – Alex Muirhead.  39 both and 40 top – Ronald Stodart. 53 both – Robert S Fairley.
35 lower, 29 both, 40 middle – Ronald Scott. 30 lower, 36 middle– James Turner.
63 top Hamilton Advertiser.

© 2010 Kenneth Liddell & Alex F. Young
First Published in the United Kingdom, 2010
Stenlake Publishing Limited
54-58 Mill Square, Catrine, KA5 6RD
01290 551122
www.stenlake.co.uk

ISBN 9781840335118

## Bibliography

David MacGibbon and Thomas Ross, *The Castellated and Domestic Architecture of Scotland – from the 12th to the 18th Century* (volume two), David Douglas, Edinburgh, 1887.

Charles F Hoy, *The Crossford-Haslebank District*, David J Clark Ltd, Glasgow, 1946.

Thomas Johnstone, *Motherwell Memories*, Hamilton Advertiser, 1938.

Thomas Reid, *Fords, Ferries, Floats and Bridges Near Lanark*, Proceedings of the Antiquaries of Scotland, 1912-13.

# Introduction

Since Bygone Clyde Valley – the Orchard Country was first published in 1991, signs of dramatic change, bar the inevitable creep of housing into the rural idyll, have been somewhat difficult to detect. Granted, one mammoth headache for drivers at Garrion Bridge has been relieved, albeit with a significant environmental price to pay and the complete obliteration of the near three hundred year-old downstream view of the graceful spans of the old bridge. Such is progress and perhaps in the circumstances this was the least unpopular option.

In a positive vein, public access legislation has now opened up large tracts of the valley, including some of the old estates north of the river. The Clyde Walkway now links Lanark with Glasgow, and the woodlands of the Clyde, Avon and Nethan are under active care to preserve their natural habitats. Attention has now turned to what remains of the ancient orchards in an effort to both preserve and develop the patchy network into a brand which might attract commercial interest and stimulate tourism. Underpinning all this, the garden centres have adapted to attract the all-year-round tourist, eager to browse, eat and relax and they remain the biggest "draw" to the area, crucial for the developments above.

Commercial fruit production in the valley is referred to in the early seventeenth century, its origins are, however, probably earlier. At its peak in the late nineteenth century the Clyde Valley encompassed a third of Scotland's orchard acarage. In 1897, Lanarkshire was the Scottish county with the largest acarage covered by fruit production. In the 1940s the county provided two thirds of Scotland's tomato crop in its 10 million square feet of glasshouses; as a whole Scotland had 17 million square feet of glasshouses.

The Clyde Valley has in the past been simultaneously a rich source of both coal and fruit, in particular spots coexisting happily together, a union unique in Scotland. Major figures in Scotland's history have made their presence felt here…Wallace, Bruce, Scott and the Hamiltons amongst the most famous. Large country estates thrived as the coal was hewn or the steel was cast, but other more established ancient lines found the going tough, their estates passing to industrialists in search of country seats.

This expanded glimpse of the Clyde Valley embraces the river environs of Bothwell, Hamilton and Motherwell, stretching in the south east to the World Heritage village of New Lanark. The people in many of the photogrpahs of over one hundred years ago are now bereft of contemporaries who would remember them personally. One of the last of these "old timers", Janet (Jen) Murray of Dalserf, died in 2007, aged 107, and is remembered through some of her own recollections in this volume and in early Edwardian photographs reproduced herein.

Bonnington Linn (left), Corra Linn (above) together with Dundaff Linn at New Lanark form the popular attraction of the Upper Falls of Clyde. In 1927 Bonnington hydro-electric power station was built between Corra Linn and Dundaff Linn, the station draws its water from an inlet just above the Bonnington Falls. Since that time the flow of water over the falls has been reduced except for special 'Waterfall Days'. On those days the full flow of the water is allowed to make its way over the falls and returns them to their full glory.

# New Lanark

In some ways the story of the birth and growth of New Lanark goes back to the Act of Union of 1707. If not for the Union, George Dempster, M.P. for the Boroughs of Perth & Dundee, and a man set to go down in history as one of the leading "improvers" of the Scottish Enlightenment, would not have been travelling to and from Westminster. In 1783 Dempster, accompanied by his wife, was dallying amongst the scenic beauty of Derbyshire's Peak District and one day came across "a palace of enormous size, having, at least, a score of windows of a row, and five or six stories in height." This so-called palace was Richard Arkwright's cotton mill at Cromford. Dempster used his powers of persuasion to get a guided tour of the mill and then called on Arkwright at home unannounced because (as he later explained), his "curiosity could not be fully gratified without seeing the head from whence the mill had sprung". Arkwright bade him in and made him most welcome, perhaps surprisingly as Arkwright admitted to his guest that he was so devoted to his work that he couldn't abide socialising, not because he was antisocial but because he was always too busy thinking about work to bother with small talk.

Arkwright had made his fortune from his patented water frame. From 1778 this was available to other manufacturers under licence; they had to buy the machinery from him and then pay him an annual royalty on every spindle. However, by the time of Dempster's visit, enforcement had become difficult. Manufacturers in isolated locations were simply stealing the technology. Arkwright pursued breaches in court, but with only a few years before the patent was due to expire in 1789 much of his income looked set to disappear. Scotland, unlike England, had little in the way of an existing cotton industry and had plenty of very cheap and available labour thanks to the Highland and Lowland Clearances. It also had lots of potential water power thanks to the topography and the rainfall. This made Scotland ideal as a new centre of the cotton industry as with cheaper labour costs it would be able to undercut the Lancashire mills.

The bellcote atop the New Buildings, which were built as accommodation in 1798. The bell was cast in 1786 for Washington County Lutherian Congregation in America's Maryland, but ended up at New Lanark and was installed on Mill Number 1 from which it was moved in the mid 19th century.

Arkwright sought out Dempster on his next visit to London and offered to "assist" him in establishing a cotton mill in Scotland. The next year, 1784, Arkwright visited Scotland and networked with men of capital and improvers across the country. As a result of this visit a number of large cotton mills were subsequently built with Arkwright's assistance, either as a partner or as a supplier. One of the worthies Arkwright met with was David Dale, already a wealthy linen merchant and first Glasgow agent of the Royal Bank of Scotland. In 1785 Dale and Arkwright went into partnership with Dempster at New Lanark. Dale and Dempster provided capital and sourced the workforce, Arkwright supplied the technical know-how - engineers to plan and construct the water supply system, designs for buildings and machinery. Their first mill was operating by 1786 and profits flowed sufficiently to allow the building of a second mill in 1789. These boom years were brought to an abrupt halt by the outbreak of war with France in 1793 followed very quickly by the collapse of much of the Scottish economy. Businesses went bust, there was a run on coin, debts were called in and over-lending by Dale caused the near collapse of the Royal Bank of Scotland, itself only saved by government intervention. The war years were difficult and at one point Dale considered laying off hundreds of hands at New Lanark. Over the ensuing years Dale disposed of his business empire and in 1799 New Lanark was sold to a young Robert Owen and his Manchester partners and backers. Owen married Dale's daughter Caroline that September. Conditions for business almost immediately looked brighter also as the war with France ended when Napoleon seized power that November.

Productivity was low and the workforce was unhappy as many of the inhabitants had come to New Lanark not so much through choice as desperation. Owen swiftly made the changes of a new broom, with a few dismissals, the tightening up of discipline and increases in working hours. To compensate Owen extended the houses, giving families two rooms instead of one, cleaned and paved the streets and established a company store which made minimal profit. Drunkenness and "irregular intercourse between the sexes" resulted in fines paid into a community fund for the ill and the sick to which the workers also made a contribution from their wages. Output improved and so his partners went along with the social improvements. In 1806 Britain was again at war with France and an embargo of America resulted in the mills closing for over four months due to lack of raw cotton supplies but the workforce kept on at full wages. This was not only popular with the inhabitants, it was also a shrewd strategic move as a skilled mill workforce was not so easily to be found now as twenty years before. Once back in production profits flowed again. The years rolled by and Owen began to promote his beliefs and publish his idealistic views as essays entitled A New View of Society, but when he announced he was going to build a school in the village his partners felt it was a step too far. New Lanark was sent to auction, with a view to Owen being ousted and his share of the mills being acquired on the cheap, but Owen had secretly found new partners better disposed to his social experiments. The plotters against Owen had booked a celebratory banquet in anticipation of their victory but outbid instead they forlornly picked at their food in silence.

NEW LANARK

BRAXFIELD ROW
NEW LANARK

Owen built his school and New Lanark and Owen became ever more famous for its social experimentation, but in 1824 Owen left New Lanark to pursue his Utopian vision further. Thus began a different chapter in his life, itself a worthy subject of a book of its own. Owen moved to America and purchased (New) Harmony in Indiana where his experiment in community-building failed three years later. In 1829 he returned to Britain with much of his previous fortune now dissipated and returned to lecturing his Utopian beliefs. With reform in the air much of what he said resonated with the working class who now looked to him for leadership. The co-operative movement was in its infancy and this culminated in the opening of the Equitable Labour Exchange, a co-operative whereby members' labour could be swopped for the products of the labour of other trades. Modern day Lets schemes operate on the same principles.

Despite his industrialist origins history has adopted Owen as the "adored leader of the first great wave of co-operation, socialism and trade unionism in Britain". These aspects of Owen were instrumental in New Lanark being designated a World Heritage Site by UNesco in 2001, although the site's intactness as a large early cotton mill was also a contributory factor. It's unfortunate that the contributions of David Dale and his partner, Claud Alexander at New Lanark's sister mill at Catrine in Ayrshire is often neglected. Undoubtedly Owen took Dale and Alexander's existing paternalistic ideas (Alexander talks in a 1791 letter of the people of Catrine as being his "family" ) and developed them further. Owen was quite dismissive about his father-in-law's educational provision at New Lanark, but at both New Lanark and Catrine the partners had been at the cutting edge of socially enlightened management with schooling for the children and at Catrine free medical assistance and full wages for the injured, amongst other benefits. Both these places were being held up as model examples years before Owen famously arrived at New Lanark, talking about it being the place to conduct his "experiment".

After Owen's departure New Lanark's history was less eventful and in the 1880s it was sold to Henry Birkmyre's Gourock Ropework Company. The firm made textile goods for the shipping industry, including rope and canvas, and once had been the largest company in the world but production ceased in 1968. New Lanark was sold on and faced an uncertain future until being placed in public ownership in 1983 by a Compulsory Purchase Order. Almost thirty years on and after much investment from the public purse (worth every penny!) New Lanark is a significant local employer and attracts visitors from all over the world.

# Kirkfieldbank

Kirkfieldbank sprang up chiefly as a means of accommodating those awaiting to cross the Clyde. The once separate settlements of Linnville and Dublin became part of Kirkfieldbank village. This photograph shows the road south into Kirkfieldbank (now Riverside Road), passing Linnville, in the 1920s. Before the decade was out, the terrace would be demolished for three blocks of four council houses.

After descending from Linnville, the road levels and crosses the bridge over the Kirkfield Burn to pass the row of cottages at Dublin. Further along the road the factory of J & R Meikle wove skirtings and later chenille curtains and covers. The site is now occupied by Nicholson Plastics.

The Dublin Pipe Bridge, built by Lanarkshire County Council in 1935 to carry a new 24 inch water main to serve the area around Kirkfieldbank. It is a meeting place, for the pipe carries water from the Daer Reservoir, near the headstream of the River Clyde.

Dublin Row looking west, with the river to the right beyond the bushes. The 1841 Census shows that 26 of the 28 houses were occupied – 22 of them by cotton weavers, and the four others by an agricultural labourer, a bookseller, a spirit dealer and a 69 year old, worn out, army pensioner.

**The main street, south, from Agnes McGilvary's shop (with the Barr's sign) on the left and the end of Stein's Loan on the right, around 1909.**

The 'Kirkfieldbank Public Hall and Miners Welfare Institute 1926', and the ground on which it stood, was gifted to the town by Mr and Mrs A K H Stein of Kirkfield. Archibald Kenneth Hyndman Stein was the eldest of Kirkfield House and in 1900 had married Janet Wallace of Kilbank House. The family also owned the ground on which the two blocks of council houses were built and the Lanark Baptist Mission Church.

Built on ground gifted by John Stein of Kirkfield House, the foundation stone of the 400 seat Kirkfieldbank Parish Church was laid by Mrs Margaret-Mary Stein (his 24 year old daughter in law) on Friday, 11th August 1871, and the work completed the following year at a cost of £800. However, one little difficulty occurred that Friday night. As part of the ceremony, a glass jar containing that day's newspapers and contemporary coins was placed under the stone, but stolen later that night. Over the weekend, a number of boys were helping police with their enquiries. With the work completed the church was dedicated on 13th July 1872. The spire was removed in 2005, due to the potential cost of renovation work.

A late 1960s photograph, looking back to the Public Hall. The cottage on the left cannot be dated, but was last occupied by the retired chimney sweep, Andrew Graham, remembered for his prize chrysanthemums – and his humour. Next, is the Lanark Baptist Mission church, built in the late nineteenth century, and latterly in the charge of three trustees namely John Mather of Lanark, Henry Bell of New Lanark and James Greig, also of New Lanark. Membership diminished and in 1948 the building was gifted to Kirkfieldbank Parish Church.

Kirkfieldbank's main street, opening with the war memorial on the left and the Kirkfield Tavern on the right. Known localy as the "Tavern" it was refurbished as the Riverside Bar and Restaurant in 2009. During the refurbishment, a 1969 mural (4 feet by 25 feet) of the Falls of Clyde by the author and artist Alasdair Gray, was uncovered. The artist was invited to come and restore the work which he duly did. Regretably, however, at the time of writing the Riverside has ceased trading. Also on the right was the Lanark Provident Co-operative Society's shop which traded between 1902 and 1968.

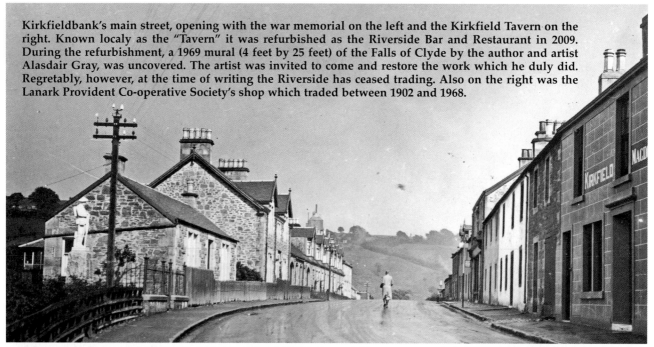

At the close of the First World War, communities across Britain formed committees to raise money to build memorials to the fallen. At Kirkfieldbank, Mr George Harvie and his committee raised sufficient funds for this memorial, unveiled by Lieutenant Colonel C J Edmonstoune Cranstoun of Corehouse on Saturday 21st October 1922. It commemorates the 26 men of the area who fell in the war. This photograph was taken later in the day, with the flowers still fresh – no poppies yet. Those killed on the battlefield lie in graveyards across northern France – Vimy, Bazentin-le-Petit, Bouchoir and Ribecourt – whilst a number died of their wounds at home. There were those reported 'missing in action', who have no headstone. The Second World War added sixteen more names, remembering not only the sergeants, corporals and private soldiers, but stokers, able bodied seamen, flying officers and flight sergeants, buried in farther-off places – Cassino, Basra and Hong Kong. Lieutenant Colonel Charles Joseph Edmonstoune Cranstoun who had served with the Lanarkshire Yeomanry and the 6th Battalion Gordon Highlanders, was twice mentioned in despatches and awarded the DSO and the French Croix de Guerre avec Palme.

The terrace of houses as the road runs down to the bridge, with the shop of the butcher and poulterer James T E Riley (who had succeeded Willie Muir in the late 1950s). That, plus the adjoining building to the right became Lovejoys, a pizza restaurant in the late 1980s/early 1990s but now gone. Lanark Gasometer can be seen to the right on the 'brae' near Steel's Cross in Lanark.

The view looking back along Main Street in 1939. The cottage on the right stood in the grounds of Annville House, home in the late nineteenth century to the draper John Brown. In 1958, Lanarkshire County Council bought and demolished it, utilising its grounds for the approach to the new bridge. Memory of the house lives on through the pages of the 2003 mystery thriller The Flourish by Canadian writer Heather Spears. The book is based on the circumstances of a double murder committed in Annville in 1883, one of the victims being an ancestor of the author. Once a prospering business, the Clyde Valley Hotel limped on through trading difficulties in the 1950s. In 1974 the name was struck off the register of companies and by the late 1980s the building lay empty. Application for demolition was eventually granted in 1992 and its replacement by a new block of flats soon followed.

*Right*: Kirkfieldbank's 'old town' rising from the bridge as the road runs out to Boathouse and Brae in the early 1890s. The houses on the left back onto the Clyde, whilst those on the right conceal the town's gas works with its two gasometers, which had been there since at least the 1850s. The railings on the right surrounded the Kirkfield Inn, later the Kirkfield Hotel.

*Below*: The old town some 20 years later. The cottages on the left have tumbled down, whilst on the right a 'Lyons Tea' sign has replaced "Barr's aerated waters". the buildings on the right, up to the white cottage were demolished in the 1950s.

Kirkfieldbank Bridge carrying the road from Lanark into the village, around 1904. Branching at the Kirkfield Hotel, the road to the left goes up the old town, whilst to the right passes along the newer part.

A 1649 proposal to bridge the Clyde at Kirkfieldbank was abandoned, and only in 1696 did the three years' work on the three-span, rubble built, bridge start, to a plan by John Lockhart of Birkenhead, Lanark. It was then known as Clydesholm Bridge, later Lanark Old Bridge and subsequently Kirkfieldbank Bridge. It still stands, but increasing motor vehicle traffic in the late 1920s and early 1930s and numerous fatalities on the brae to Lanark demanded a road alignment and a new bridge. In 1931 the county council announced their scheme to build a single skew bridge with a span of 140 feet and width of 53 feet, costing £68,000. The plan was shelved, due to a nationwide economy drive, but was looked at again in 1938 and once more abandoned. Finally the company of Murdoch McKenzie won the contract to build the new bridge (1956-1959) and on 17th April 1959, Edward Daly, Lanarkshire's County Convener, had the honour of cutting the ribbon.

The mill on the Mouse Water or, more correctly, on a lade fed by it, around 1905 when it was operated by George Thomson, the miller and grain dealer. It dates from 1719 when it was a wheat and corn mill owned by the burgesses of Lanark who, in 1795, added a barley mill. By 1913 its milling days were over, and it was sold as a seven acre orchard and market garden. In December 1984, Clydesdale District Council granted planning permission to convert the mill to two dwellinghouses.

Kirkfield House, once part of Stonebyres estate, was bought by John Stein, a landed proprietor, and son of Andrew Stein, a distiller in the Alloa area, in 1834. On his death it fell to his son Archibald Hyndman Stein, an advocate who in 1870 married 23 year old Margaret Mary Anderson, daughter of Patrick Anderson, late minister of the Congregational Church at New Lanark. By 1881 they were living at Kirkfield House with their three sons, John (9), Archibald (4) and Andrew (4 months), and five servants and a coachman in the gatehouse. Comprising of three public rooms, three bedrooms, laundry and servant's room, it stood in an acre of garden well stocked with fruit trees. Archibald, Senior passed away in 1911 and Margaret died in January 1938 at Hagg's Road, Glasgow at the advanced age of 91 years. The last of the Stein line died in Australia in 1990.

The road from Kirkfieldbank, at the gatehouse to Sunnyside Lodge, before branching left for Nemphlar and right for Cartland Bridge.

# Stonebyres

Stonebyres Linn photographed in the year prior to the building of the power station that would utilise its energy. It has two main ledges of rock, old red sandstone, taking the river down 69 feet to the Salmon Pool.

Stonebyres Power Station, with another at Bonnington, was built in 1926 by Sir William Arrol & Co., and commissioned the following year, for the Clyde Valley Electrical Power Company. They are now the oldest hydro-electric power stations in the United Kingdom, and served as models for later schemes. Each station had two turbines. These and the electrical plant were supplied by the English Electric Co. of Preston in Lancashire. Water was brought into the power station by means of a weir, pipeline and tunnel, from 90 feet above the generator house, where it drove two turbines at 375 revolutions per minute, the 11,000 volt generator producing 3.2 megawatts of electricity.

Prior to the 1840s, Stonebyres House was a simple fifteenth century tower house measuring 34 feet by 29 feet and owned by the family Vere, later Weir. The 860 acre estate and mansion house was advertised for sale in 1833 as 'one of the oldest and most venerable edifices in the county … the whole fit for the accommodation of a genteel family', and again in 1839. It was bought by the Glasgow wine merchant James Monteath, who engaged the Glasgow architect John Baird to convert it to a 'modern' mansion with extensive additions. More work followed in 1845. James N Graham of Carfin bought it in 1906 and by 1914 had spent over £60,000 on further renovations and extensions, but never occupied it. He sold it back to the Monteaths in 1924. Following the annual Lanark County Ball in September 1934, it was sold to J F Lamonby of Uddingston, for £1,750. He demolished it and sold off the fixtures and fittings – oak parquet flooring, drawing room fittings, mahogany panelled billiard room, electric lift (unused), a large Wellstood kitchen range, electric fittings, doors, windows and fancy stonework, all to be cleared, he advertised, at low prices.

Stonebyres School on the Auchenheath road was built in 1829 on land granted by Daniel Vere of Stonebyres to serve the village, and surrounding area, of Hazelbank and was in use until around 1877 when the pupils were transferred to Underbank Public School. Its last master was Thomas Affleck, who served from the late 1840s, living in the part of the building nearest the camera with his second wife, Jane Tennant, whom he had married in 1841 and, latterly, three children. He died, at the schoolhouse, in June 1881, whilst she died there in 1903 – the year this photograph was taken.

# Hazelbank

A 1902 view from the hillside above Hazelbank. On the left is Hazelbank Brae, with Broomhouse, occupied by 35 year old traction engine driver, John Wallace and his family, and Alderbank, home to 38 year old John Clelland, a fruit grower. Nestling amongst the trees to the right is Orchardville. Built around 1803 by a Mr Thomson who, according to Charles F Hoy's book The Crossford-Hazelbank District, named it Hazelbank Cottage, lending the name to the settlement. When photographed it was home to 57 year old, London born, Emma Trovell, who termed herself a fruit grower, and her 87 year old aunt Janet Waugh, widow of John H W Waugh, who owned the property.

An original copy of this 1900 photograph is inscribed; Mr & Mrs Crosbie's cottage, Hazelbank, referring to Robert Crosbie and his wife Laura (nee Brown), who had married in Glasgow in May 1893. He had been a 33 year old fruit grower, living at Corra, and she a 29 year old mantle maker from Glasgow's King Street. They now had four children; Robert (7), Nellie (6), Alexander (3) and Thomas (1). They too, like Christina Gray in the post office had two lunatics living with them, at least on the night of the 1901 Census , 69 year old Christina Currie from Glasgow, and Jane Brown aged 64 years from Campsie in Stirlingshire.

The medley of houses along the Lanark Road through Hazelbank speaks of a slow development over many decades. By the 1880s most were occupied by miners and their families, as new coal mines and quarries opened both within the surrounding area and beyond.

The Post Office at Hazelbank around 1903 with children, and a cart, out for the photographer. The post mistress was Christina Gray, a widow in her mid forties who had run the shop as a general store until Hazelbank was granted sub-post office status in February 1899. With her in the three apartment house were her 14 year old daughter Margaret, a school monitor, and a son and daughter, both scholars. Also in the house were three 'feeble minded' boarders, two from Glasgow and one from Carluke.

The house with Hazelbank's, re-sited, post office in the 1920s, when occupied by the fruit grower, William Robertson and his post mistress wife Agnes (nee Gracie). The post box was removed many years ago, leaving a cement outline on the wall. The Robertsons later moved to Stevenston on the Ayrshire coast, where William became a foreman at the Nobel Explosives Factory, and where Agnes died as an 81 year old widow, in January 1950. The identities of the women in the photograph are not known but one of them inscribed on the rear of the photograph, " … *we were out watching a motor car when we were caught, so don't laugh*". When the house was bought, and renovated, in the early 1960s, the well-worn linoleum in the rear middle bedroom, the onetime post office and general shop, was a medley of patches.

# Nemphlar

Nemphlar's grocer's shop and post office with, perhaps, the proprietress Christina Lockhart Scott in the doorway. The man's name is unknown but, perhaps was her son William Scott, born 1877. The daughter of John Main, a cotton weaver of Halcrofthead, Nemphlar, she was born in 1834 and was the village grocer when she married 40 year old cotton weaver, Thomas Scott in February 1876. He died in 1891, leaving her to carry on the business until she passed away in 1905.

The Education (Scotland) Act 1872 introduced compulsory education for children between the ages of 5 and 13 years and brought on a rush of new school building. In October 1873, Sir Simon Macdonald Lockhart, Baronet of Lee and Carnwath, offered Lanark Landward School Board two sites, one at Nemphlar and the other at Cartland, for their new schools. The architect Hugh Marr of Lanark was engaged, and the building tenders were advertised in June 1875. Marr had been Lord Cornet to Lanark's Lanimer celebrations in 1836. The builder is not known. At the end of 1885 Nemphlar School had a roll of 47 and an average attendance of 34. At the time of this 1912 photograph the headmistress was Miss Lyle, assisted by Miss Murphy, teaching 48 children. The school closed in 1966.

# Carfin

Carfin House in the summer of 1911, when home to James Noble Graham and his family. He had bought it in 1880 from Gavin Steel, changing the name from Holmhead to Carfin, and although this structure dates only from the early nineteenth century, the estate's roots go back over many centuries to a family Nisbet. The estate extended to 300 acres, of which 108 were woodland and rough uncultivated land and 32 acres were parkland. The house had six public rooms, five large bedrooms, eight small bedrooms, eight attic rooms, three bathrooms and ample servant's quarters and, by the 1920s, was lit by acetylene gas. Graham, of the wine importers W & J Graham, died in Portugal in October 1928. The house was demolished in 1957 and in 1989 the Clyde Valley Country Estate (now Valley International Park) opened as a visitor centre.

The suspension footbridge into Carfin estate from Underbank, opposite the old school, was supplied and built, in the late 1880s, by P & R Fleming & Co. of 29 Argyle Street, Glasgow for Graham of Carfin House, superseding the ford. The super-structure above the centre pier has a gate. The bridge was fully restored one hundred years later to serve the needs of the country estate.

# Braidwood

Standing to the east of the Braidwood road, the five storey, rubble built, fortalice, Hallbar Tower dates from the 1530s when a government directive obliged land owners with estates valued over £100 to build protective towers against incursions from Border raiders. It is 58 feet high, and 24 feet square, with five feet thick walls. In 1581 the Barony of Braidwood was transferred to Harie Stewart of Gogar, passed to Lord Maitland of Thirlestane in Berwickshire and was in the hands of the Marquis of Douglas by 1681 before passing to Sir George Lockhart of Lee Castle. This photograph dates from around 1903.

Mashock Mill, off the Braidwood road, around 1900, when it was surrounded by fields of fruit. The house and cornmill date to the seventeenth century when it was a thatched, three storey building, and worked as a mill until the 1870s.

# Crossford

The extensive greenhouses of Forrest Brothers' nursery at Crossford were started around 1905 by Thomas Forrest, then a 55 year old fruit merchant. The business took in his sons David, John, Thomas, Manson and Robert. In the open ground to the right they grew raspberries and gooseberries, along with pears and apples, but their business expanded with the cultivation of tomatoes. Over the summer the plants were tended and harvested before being cleared out to allow steam sterilising, for the following year.

The road from the north sweeping into Crossford, with Kate Frame's shop on the left, in the 1920s. The next two cottages survive, but the ones beyond were demolished for the opening of Smuggler's Brig Road. The village's two churches stood on the left – the United Secession Church with the steeple, founded in 1832 (United Presbyterian from 1847) and, with its belfry, the Free Church of Scotland (1870). The Free and the U.P. Churches amalgamated in 1900, but only on 10th July 1918 did the congregations in Crossford unite. In 1929 the congregation returned to the Church of Scotland.

In August 1912 the macadamised road was metalled and tarred. Crossford's popularity for 'days out' in the 1920s brought a rush of tea rooms and 'ices and chips' shops, also business for Campbell's Garage through the sale of petrol.

John Thomson attending a motorist outside his tearoom in the summer of 1911. A 36 year old grocer, he had recognised the growth of tourism through the valley, and capitalised on it. He lived at Rankinland, Crossford, with his wife Martha, ten years his senior, whom he had married in 1898. In 1895 he was elected to the county council as the representative for Kirkfieldbank, beating James Graham Gilchrist the fruit grower from Hazelbank by 191 votes to 134. Thomson retired in the late 1930s and Robert Miller converted the business to a fish and chip shop.

The view north, with Frame, the carriage hirer's premises, Meadow Bank, on the left and the United Presbyterian Church on the right.

The main street around 1910, looking north from Sandy's Well on the left and Holm Road, with Capie the butcher's shop, on the right.. The adjacent building has the date stone 'D T 1833' on the pediment, perhaps referring to the stone mason David Thomson of Hazelbank, and was the first in this terrace to be built. Beyond it is the Carluke Co-operative Society premises, managed by Henry Flemington, down to the opening for Chalmers the joiner.

The semi-detached Sandy's Well Cottage above and behind the spring in the 1890s, with Meg Fairley, outside her shop on the left, and Jimmy Dewar standing to the right.

Crossford and Hazelbank War Memorial was dedicated by the Reverend Alex Sutherland, when unveiled by James Noble Graham, on Sunday 21st May 1922. A committee had raised £340 and engaged local builder and sculptor Robert Speedie – born in Holm Road in 1883 – to execute the work, choosing Sandy's Well as its site. Amongst the twenty fallen was Graham's son, Captain William Lovett Cameron Graham of the Indian Army Reserve, killed at Bombay in July 1915, whilst disembarking troops from the hospital ship *Madras*. At the end of the Second World War a further ten names were added, and in the 1950s two more, one from the Korean War and one from the Malaysian conflict.

The war memorial a few years after its unveiling with two boys collecting water. Domestic tap water was available from the summer of 1924, but not every house would take it. The boy to the right, with the jug, is thought to be William Watson, a future blacksmith. Behind the monument, Sandy's Well Cottage is on the left and the manse is on the right. In the 1990s the water from the spring stopped flowing and in 2000 the Millennium Committee through the War Memorial Restoration Group undertook the project to raise funds to restore the water and replace the name plaques. Work commenced in 2008 and was completed in spring 2010 at a cost of £23,000.

James and Mary Robertson (nee McDill) of Sandy's Well Cottage with their 18 month old son Alexander, at the war memorial in 1929. They had married in Glasgow in January 1927 when he was a 35 year old coal miner living in Crossford and she a 32 year old domestic servant with Lord Clydesmuir at Braidwood House. They had two daughters, Lizzie (1928) and Mary (1933). James left the pits and worked for Adam Stewart, who had taken over Leiper's bakery.

The Crossford based football club Clydeside Rovers in the spring of 1922, after winning the Menzies Cup (a South Lanarkshire Juvenile League competition) by beating a team from Douglas Water. The cup had been put up by Sir Walter Menzies, the Liberal MP for South Lanarkshire. The players are;

**Front row (left to right)**; Jim Robertson (outside right), Donald McAdam (inside right),
Alex Reid (centre forward), Jim Muir (inside left) and David Paterson (outside left).
**Centre row**; Willie Rankin (right half), John Wilson (centre half) and George Orr (left half);
**Back row**; George McAdam (trainer), Andrew Muir (right back), Willie Graham (goal keeper),
John McArthur (left back), Jock Gray (Manager) and Alex McCulloch (trainer).

Founded in 1919, as were many others in the post-war period (540 teams entered the initial draw for the Scottish Juvenile Cup in 1920-21) their home pitch was on top of the disused Annabella Bing (previously home to Craignethan Thistle). They played in the Auchenheath and District League, but disbanded in, or around, 1926.

The butcher Thomas Russell Capie outside his premises on the Holm Road corner, around 1918. Born 'above the shop' in Main Street, Kirkfieldbank in 1888, his father, William Capie was the butcher there, with a branch in Lanark's Bloomgate Street. He traded here for a number of years, retiring to Lanark's Delves Road where he died in 1958, aged 70 years.

Holm Road looking to Main Street around 1920. It is not known when the road was built, but was clearly made to join the road from Nethanfoot as it made for the ferry crossing. Today, the war memorial can be seen from here, and the tenement and thatched cottage on the right have been replaced with modern buildings.

Holm Road, now running parallel to the river with the grounds of Clydevale on the right, as it heads for Nethanfoot Bridge. The two cottages on the left are gone, the second of which, with its corrugated iron roof, was home to Jeannie Robertson.

Main Street with a group on the right who are outside John Robertson the draper's shop. One of them is seated on the large piece of coal which was there for many years. Sometime in the 1870s there was a competition to raise the most neatly hewn cubic yard of coal from local mines and this piece of cannel coal, from Blair Braes pit on the Nethan, was entered by Andrew Rankine and David Copland of Hazelbank, coming second to a piece from an Auchenheath pit raised by Gavin Baxter. Today (2010) it stands, at a higher level, in the 'Forrest' .

The view south along Main Street around 1900. The licensee of the Crossford Inn (established in the 1850s) was Carluke born Mary Ann Thomson who had succeeded her husband George on his death in October 1895. There was stabling to the rear and, in summer, she supplied picnic parties with hampers, and there was trout fishing in the river at the foot of the garden. Next, on the Braidwood Road corner, is the 1876 built Lanarkshire Constabulary police station, comprising of a very small 'police office' with one cell and a kennel to the rear, with a living room and two bedrooms, with kitchen, for the constable and his family. When photographed it was occupied by Banffshire born Constable James Cowie and his wife Helen. An indication of the nomadic life of a county policeman shows in the birthplaces of his five children. The two eldest were born in Shettleston, the second and third in Cambuslang and the fifth in Lesmahagow. The last constable to live here was John Shearer, with his wife Nancy. Transferred from Strathaven in October 1968, he served from here until the opening of the new station on Graham Road in 1974, and retired in October 1979. On the opposite corner is James Leiper's shop, as the view looks up to his home, Drumassie House.

James Leiper's bakery shop on the Braidwood Road corner around 1903 with an assistant, and dog, in the doorway. The 1841 Census shows John Leiper as a 31 year old baker, living in the village with his wife Mary, his six children, a journeyman baker and two apprentice bakers. Mary died and in December 1863, 54 year old John, now a baker and landed proprietor, married 41 year old farmer's daughter, Isabella Farrie. Their son, James, who would carry on the bakery business, was born the following April. John died in February 1888. In 1890 James married Kate Scott, daughter of the preserve manufacturer Robert Scott. He died in February 1939, his death certificate showing him as a fruitgrower.

**The bridge carrying the Braidwood road into Crossford, with aprons on the washing line behind Leiper the baker's premises.**

Two miners, by the names of Weir and Dyer, are thought to have started strawberry growing in Crossford. Fruit grower Alexander Scott supervising the springtime weeding of Manse Park, a strawberry field on the 23 acre Flatt Farm, overlooking Crossford, around 1910. The farm was owned by his father, James Templeton Scott, and had been in the family since 1802. In 1911 Alexander married Martha Hamilton of Mossbank Cottage, Lesmahagow, in Crossford's Free Church manse. She is thought to be one of the women in the photograph. The sunbonnets worn by the women were known as crazies.

**James and Alexander Scott, sons of James Templeton Scott of Flatt Farm, in the early 1900s, filling their back pack sprayers with insecticide.**

*Right*: Built by the baker James Leiper around 1902, Drumassie stands on the family's 22 acre Bankend Farm, under the 'Stairheid Knowe', which rises behind the house. At the rear and side of Drumassie, the self-explanatory and ancient 'Coo' Road climbs towards its former destination at Auchenheath. Its accommodation comprised of a lounge, dining room, four bedrooms and a maid's room. It was later occupied by Dr John McCallum Lang, until his death in June 1950.

*Below*: David Brown and David Robertson, workers from Flatt Farm, with their strawberry barrows, after dispatching a load of fruit to market. Below Drumassie, James Scott of Flatt Farm sits in the Singer motor car, he had converted to a pick-up.

**Main Street from Drumassie with Bankend, Leiper's farmhouse, on the left, and the tenement block, demolished to make way for Forrest Place, on the right.**

The village main street, photographed from Stairheid Knowe. The hayshed in the earlier upper view was replaced by Drumassie. The bridge was built under an act of 1834 and managed by Crossford Bridge Trust, which was also responsible for 300 yards of road on either side. The building cost was covered by £850 from subscribers and a loan of £1,800 which was paid off in August 1858. The pontage was let for £300 in 1856-57, falling to £151 for 1857-58 and reduced again to £108 for the following year – due to the loss of coal traffic to the Lesmahagow Railway.

Once part of Carfin Estate's Davingill Wood, Crossford Public Park opened in May 1930. The trees were cleared, the ground was prepared, and its paths cut, before the children's swings were fixed to their concrete bases and the flower beds planted. Today it has a few more shrubs but no (dangerous!) swings.

The road to Lanark approaching the bridge over the Davin Burn with Underbank Public School, on the right, through the arch of trees. When abandoned as a school in 1925 the building took on many guises, serving many purposes. Not surprisingly it became, firstly, a community hall until the Second World War when it was a displaced persons shelter. Gilmour the coal merchant used it as a depot. Through the late 1970s and early 80s it was home to the Clydeside Trading Company and in 1990, the Old School Restaurant and, finally, in 1998 became a dwellinghouse.

The school, and its roll of 280 pupils, was divided into three sections; the Infant Room (Wee End), the Class Room (Middle End) and the School Room (Big End).

Robert Shand Dewar, was the school headmaster for 33 years. Born in Perth in 1849, he started his teaching career at Auchtergaven School, north of Perth, in 1867, and served three years at Ruthvenfield School from 1869. In 1872 he married Helen Stewart Chalmers before transferring to Glasgow's Langside Academy. Graduating from Glasgow University in 1879, he applied to fill the vacant post at Underbank Public School at £100 per annum, with fees for special subjects and evening classes and was successful. He had come at a bad time. In June 1878, H. M. Inspector of Schools had reported, "This school has decidedly fallen off since last inspection … Throughout the various standards there was a high percentage of failures and, in addition, the work lacked style in execution. … by the next inspection matters will be remedied". Dewar, remembered as 'the genial dictator', soon remedied the faults and earned favourable future reports. He retired in December 1912, moving to Smith Street, in Glasgow's Whiteinch, where he died in January 1922, aged 73 years.

Robert Dewar and his assistant, James G Baillie, who joined the school in 1880, were members of Lanark Cycling Club, but Dewar appears to have moved up from pedal to petrol power with this Minerva motor cycle, manufactured by the world's then premier motor cycle company based in Berchem, close to Antwerp, Belgium. The registration mark V 88 was issued in January or February 1904. Standing in the school gateway is (probably), his daughter Barbara born in 1876.

*Right*: School boards were introduced by the Education (Scotland) Act of 1872, with the 48 in Lanarkshire being responsible for the education of 101,848 children. This photograph shows Lesmahagow School Board, in 1911, which had responsibility for Underbank. It comprised of;

**Front row (left to right)**: John Peat Young, farmer, Kirkmuirhill Farm; W G Gallaher; Kerr A Smith, (Chairman of the Board), solicitor; and James Nisbet Gilmore, (Clerk to the Board), architect, Friars Park Lesmahagow.

**Back row**: Robert Scott of Lesmahagow, John S Groves, miner, Kirkmuirhill; Walter Forrest Jr. , fruit grower and Robert Pate, farmer, South Draffan Farm, Lesmahagow.

*Below*: A class of 12 year olds at old Underbank Public School in 1924 and soon to move to the new school, with their headmaster, Mr John M Thomson.

**Front row (left to right)**; John Paterson, Lawrence Robertson, Matthew McFarlane, James Caig, George Morton, James Scott and Archie Brown.

**Second row**; Margaret Marshall, Ella McNee, Nell Buchanan, Martha Kyle, Jemima McMahon, Annie Robertson, Martha Rankin, and Annie Gracie.

**Third row**; John Watson, Nellie Murphy, Esther Dewar, Nell Thomson, Kate McGill, Jean Marshall, Margaret Walker and Nannie Brown.

**Back row**; Robert Bryson, Sam Morrison, William Bankier, William Gray, Tom Baxter, Lawrence Walker, James Caldwell and William Prasher.

The present Underbank School was opened on Wednesday, 23rd December 1925, by Provost Peter MacAuslan of Lanark, at a ceremony conducted by Lanarkshire Education Authority's chairman, Sir Henry Shanks Keith. The need for a new school was recognised in 1914, but the war intervened and had only now come to fruition. Designed by the County Architect, John Stewart , who was also master of works, the 250 pupil school cost £7,000 with an additional £1,300 for the master's two public, three bedroom and scullery house. Both were built by Robert Speedie of Crossford, who had built the war memorial.

# Craignethan / Tillietudlem

Opened by the Caledonian Railway on 1st October 1876, Tillietudlem Railway Station was on the Motherwell-Lesmahagow branch line to the west of Craignethan Castle and was particularly busy with day trippers visiting the ruins over the summer. It closed in January 1941, but re-opened in May 1945 before finally closing in October 1951.

A group in front of the Towerhouse at Craignethan Castle, a popular outing, with Tillietudlem Railway Station only a half mile away. In those days even the grounds were in a ruinous state. A fortified manor house, building was begun around 1530 by Sir James Hamilton of Finnart, Master of Works to King James V, who also fortified Blackness Castle on the Firth of Forth. Hamilton fell from favour and was beheaded in 1540, and the castle reduced to a ruin in 1579 to prevent its use as a refuge. The name Tillietudlem comes from Sir Walter Scott's novel *Old Mortality* (published 1816), which was inspired by Craignethan Castle.

The Tillietudlem Hotel at the Blair Road junction, north of Crossford, was built by the Carluke born carpenter John Cleland and opened in 1879. It was an ideal situation, attracting custom from passing traffic, offering accommodation for visitors to Craignethan Castle and the Nethan Valley, and to fruit buyers in the autumn. The stone was quarried at Threepwood Farm and Cleland supplied the wood. He had married 20 year old Margaret Cooper in 1871 and when he died in the spring of 1884, she married another joiner, James Chalmers, in February 1885. A succession of managers were employed at the hotel meantime, but in 1901 Margaret took charge with her son, James Cleland, acting as bookkeeper. Margaret retired in 1903 and was succeeded as proprietor by her son John.

James Cleland, outside the Tillietudlem Hotel around 1903. In May 1905 he and his brother John made the national press. The hotel was lit by acetylene gas, produced on the premises, and having gone into the generator room, James was followed by his brother John lighting his way with a burning match. The resulting explosion seriously injured both of them.

A party of ladies arriving at Tillietudlem Hotel in 1904, one of them – according to the inscription on the rear of the photograph – being Aunt Mary. They would probably have come by train to Tillietudlem Station, and from there by the carriage hirer William Frame of Meadowbank, Crossford.

The bridge over the Nethan at Nethanfoot, from the north, as the road runs into Crossford, as it would have been seen in the late 1930s. Although little more than a stream the Nethan rises at 1550 feet, close to the Ayrshire border, taking a meandering 13 mile path to the Clyde, joining it a little upstream of Smuggler's Ford. The small community had developed around coal mines and a sawmill. In recent times housing development has drawn it closer to Crossford – and given us a bridge we cross without noticing.

# Waygateshaw

Wygateshaw House. Waygateshaw is first recorded as 'Wygetshaw' in a charter of 1327-8, with a land transfer from Robert Bruce to Hugo Polay. By 1539 the Lockhart family had acquired the lands on the Clyde's north bank and proceeded to build a five-storey tower house. Much of this remains, periodically restored and eventually augmented and surrounded by a Victorian mansion, designed by William Burn for Samuel Steel in 1829. The Steels in 1744 followed several generations of the Lockhart and later the Weir families in holding Waygateshaw. Samuel Steel, a county magistrate, succeeded to the estate in 1830. In 1992 fire destroyed most of the interior of the 'B' listed mansion house. Restoration was in a contemporary style save for the incorporation of a Burn fireplace from the ruins of Milton Lockhart House.

A Mulready envelope, sent to Samuel Steel Esquire of Waygateshaw in 1842 when he was a land tax commissioner for Lanarkshire. A prepaid communication, similar to the later aerogram, the Mulready envelope was introduced by Rowland Hill in May 1840 together with the Penny Black and the Two Penny blue postage stamps, designed by the Irishman, William Mulready. It features Britannia with Asia to the left and America to the right – and the happy recipients of the letters below. The idea was not a success and later abandoned.

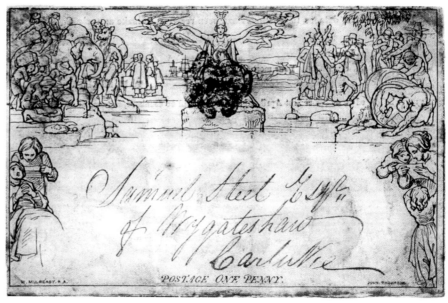

# Milton Lockhart

Designed by the Edinburgh architect William Burn, Milton Lockhart House was built between 1829 and 1836 for John Gibson Lockhart. Lockhart was a biographer – *A Life of Robert Burns* (1828), *A Life of Napoleon Buonaparte* (1829) and *Memoirs of the Life of Scott* (1837-1838) and critic, and in 1820 married Sophia Charlotte Scott, eldest daughter of Sir Walter Scott, who is said to have selected the position of the house. It remained in the family until 1951 when it was sold by Stephen Alexander Lockhart. In 1988 it was bought by the Japanese actor Masahiko Tsugawa – star of the cinema classics; *Crazed Fruit, The Funeral* and *A Taxing Woman* – who had it dismantled, transported by rail to Japan and rebuilt, along with a German village, as part of the Marble Village outside Takayamamura in rural Gunma Prefecture, 100 miles north west of Tokyo and indeed miles from anywhere.

Peter Christison came to Milton Lockhart from Ashiestiel Estate near Galashiels as head gardener in 1926, occupying the gardener's cottage. His son John, who lived there with his parents until they left in 1949, recalls the kitchen garden at the stables; peas, cabbage, cauliflower and carrots were all supplied to the "big hoose". The formal gardens were opened regularly to the public, the highlights being the Bluebell Walk and the Triangle of Rhodedendrons. This view shows staff from an earlier decade. The photograph is by Miss Agnes R. Orrock, who ran her business from Station Road, Carluke between 1907 and 1914.

# Milton Lockhart Lodge / Mauldslie Castle

Built in the early nineteenth century, and modelled on Bothwell Bridge, the three arched Milton Bridge, with gatehouse, carried the driveway into Milton Lockhart's estate. As with Mauldslie, the gates were manufactured at Walter MacFarlane's Saracen Works in Saracen Lane, Gallowgate, Glasgow, although currently they are in better condition. A short distance upstream, on the south bank, stood the corn mill, Clydes Mill.

The gatehouse and bridge to Mauldslie Castle from the north bank of the river, within the estate. It has been presumed that the gatehouse, with its date of 1861, is contemporary with the bridge but, although the bridge appears on the 1859 Ordnance Survey map, the lodge house does not. Prior to the bridge, the south access to the estate was by a ford close to Rosebank.

*Opposite top*: The lodge house and gateway at the Lanark road entrance to the estate in the early 1900s when occupied by Mary Hamilton, described in the 1901 Census as a 55 year old, widowed, lodge keeper. Above the arched gateway is the armorial plaque of the Hoziers, with its motto 'Aye Ready', whilst above the doorway at the base of the tower are the initials of James Hozier. The structure bears the date 1861, and is thought to be also the work of the architect David Bryce of Edinburgh, who designed the house. The cast iron gates were supplied by Walter MacFarlane's Saracen Works, Glasgow. Trees still thrive, but the ivy on the tower has long since been removed.

Building work on the original Mauldslie Castle started with the architect Robert Adam laying the foundation stone in 1791 and his assistant Andrew Cairns finishing the work in 1796, for Thomas Carmichael, 5th Earl of Hyndford, who died there, unmarried, in 1811. He was succeeded by his brother Andrew, 6th Earl (1758-1817). The ground floor consisted of a large entrance hall, the dining room, the drawing room, a library, and the family bedroom, with dressing rooms, whilst the second floor had six bedrooms. James Hozier, a maltman and magistrate in Glasgow, purchased the estate in 1838, and in 1860 engaged the Edinburgh architect David Bryce to add the Scottish Baronial front.

The Right Honourable James Henry Cecil Hozier, 2nd
Baron Newlands, photographed for the 1911-1912 edition
of Thomas Stothers' magazine Glasgow, Lanarkshire and
Renfrewshire, to celebrate his 60th birthday. Born at
Tannochside House (formerly St Enoch's Hall), between
Uddingston and Bellshill, on 4th April 1851, he was the
son of William Wallace Hozier, 1st Baron Newlands
(created 1898), and Frances Anne O'Hara. On 24th May
1880 he married Lady Mary Louisa Wellesley Cecil,
daughter of the 3rd Marquis of Exeter. He was private
secretary to the Marquis of Salisbury, who was Foreign
Secretary, between 1878 and 1880 and again in 1885-86
when the marquis became Prime Minister. He entered
parliament in 1886, as member for South Lanarkshire until
1906 when he succeeded to the title as 2nd Baron
Newlands, on the death of his father, William Wallace
Hozier. A member of the Royal Company of Archers, he
was Lord Lieutenant of Lanarkshire from 1915 until 1921,
when he took up residence in Brighton. The title became
extinct at his death in September 1929. The contents of the
house were auctioned in 1933 and it was demolished in the
spring of 1934. Within two years Lanarkshire County
Council had started work on a new sewage purification
works in the grounds.

Lord Newlands (there in his capacity as Lord Lieutenant of
Lanarkshire) and Lieutenant James Martin, M.C., at Carluke
Railway Station on Saturday 1st February 1919, as the town
celebrated its second Victoria Cross winner, Sergeant-Major
Thomas Caldwell of the 12th (Ayrshire and Lanarkshire
Yeomanry) Royal Scots Fusiliers. On 31st October 1918, whilst in
charge of a Lewis gun section clearing a farmhouse near
Audenarde in Belgium, 24 year old Caldwell had single-handedly
rushed the building and taken eighteen prisoners. Lieutenant
Martin of the Highland Light Infantry had been rescued by Lance
Corporal William Angus, earning him the town's previous
Victoria Cross at Givenchy in France on 12th June 1915.

Lady Newlands, Mary Louisa Wellesley Cecil, was born in July 1857 and married James Henry Cecil Hozier on 24th May 1880. She died in August 1930 and was laid to rest, with her husband, his parents and a number of the Earls of Hyndford, in the vault of Kenneth's Tower in the grounds of Mauldslie Castle.

On 12th October 1914 the Scottish Red Cross Transport Committee, in co-operation with the Royal Scottish Automobile Club, issued an appeal for motor ambulance transport which was urgently needed at the front. Lord Newlands, present at the Glasgow meeting, announced his intentions to contribute a fully-equipped motor ambulance to be sent to the front. The Newlands ardently supported the war effort; they made the Lady Hozier Convalescent Home in Lanark available for the retuning wounded and in 1915 raised £3,900 by auctioning a Stradivarius violin. Mauldslie No. 37 was one of 134 donated Scottish Red Cross ambulances employed during the First World War and was a conversion of a Singer motor car. Seven such ambulances were donated from Lanarkshire at this time. The white rails in the background may be on the racecourse at Rouen, where the Scottish Branch of the Red Cross set up and maintained a 270 bed "Scottish" hospital.

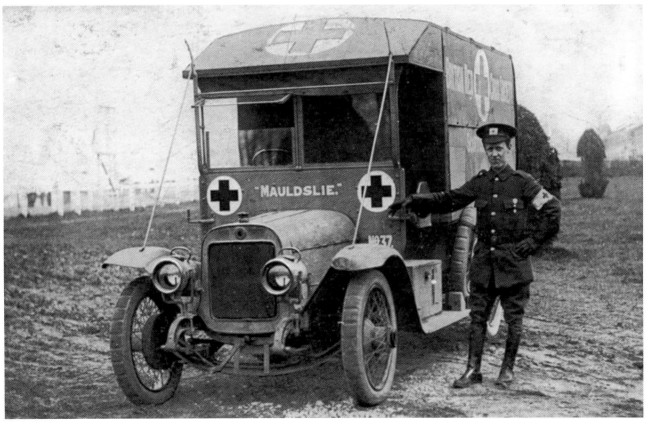

# Rosebank

Rosebank developed around the inn as a village which supported the needs of the adjoining Mauldslie Estate. A deficiency in the supply and quality of the housing stock in Dalserf also fueled the growth of Rosebank. By the time of the New Statistical Account in 1842 the village boasted 176 individuals in 24 dwelling houses.

The Rosebank Inn, on its corner site in the 1890s was soon to give way to the Popinjay Hotel. It is not known when the inn was established, but the Census of 1841 shows 45 year old Andrew Scoular as the inn keeper. Sometime in the 1870s it was taken over by John McQueen, a Crawfordjohn born ex-miner from Southfield Row, Lesmahagow, and his wife Christina, whom he had married in 1855. The business prospered, but John's previous occupation caught up with him, and he died in September 1886 of Miner's Asthma (Pneumoconiosis). Christina carried on, helped by their daughters Janet and Jeanie, and saw the building transformed into the Popinjay Hotel in 1900. She died there in May 1905.

The stone villa on the left, Rosebank Hall, was gifted to the community in 1876 by James Hozier of Mauldslie in memory of his wife Catherine Margaret Feilden, whom he had married in 1824 and who died in April 1870. It served the community as a church hall and library, and the caretaker around this time, in the early 1900s, was Marion Baker. Beyond Rosebank Hall, and the entrance to Annsfield, is the terrace of houses built in the same Tudor style as the Popinjay.

In 1899 William Wallace Hozier, 1st Baron Newlands commissioned the Hamilton based architect Alexander Cullen to redesign Rosebank village. In 1889, Cullen had reconstructed The Ross for Col. H H Robertson Aikman. The plans for the Popinjay Hotel were exhibited at the Royal Glasgow Institute of the Fine Arts in September 1901.

# Dalserf

Dalserf's Smithy, *Whindyke* on the south side of the Lanark Road and a few hundred yards west of Dalserf's Kirk Road, around 1902. It was home to 75 year old Agnes Clarke *nee* Scoular, widow of blacksmith John Clarke who had died in December 1895. She had kept the business on with her son William and by employing other blacksmiths, hence, perhaps, the cart on the roadway outside. William later worked at Rosebank. She died at Hillhead, Glasgow in 1908, aged 82 years.

Two ploughs working a field on the 125 acre Auldton Farm, part of Dalserf estate, with the Clyde winding below them. Each of these men could plough one acre per day. The ground to the right drops down to the old mill on the Lanark road, whilst across the water, but still on the south side, is the four acre steading, the Boathouse to the west of Dalserf.

A cyclist making his way out the Lanark road, approaching the Dalserf junction, with The Old Inn, home to the fruit grower Robert Sommerville Fairley on his right. The road was widened in 1925, and the trees on the right were re-planted after being felled for pit props at the close of the First World War. The Old Inn is of uncertain date, but was a coaching inn from perhaps the sixteenth century. The four stall stable and tack room survive.

Fruit pickers harvesting Victoria plums on Robert Sommerville Fairley's, eight acre Dalserf Orchard in the autumn of 1942. They were (on the ladders, left to right): Robert Smeillie, Mauldslie Stables; John Thomson, Rosebank; foreman Johnnie Watson; unknown. Standing below, to gather the fruit: John Dunn, Larkhall; Beanie Jarvis, Cornsilloch; Nan Morrison, Ashgill and Peggy Woods, also of Ashgill. There would also be four or five women employed on grading and packing. The harvest ran for three weeks through September and produced, on average, ten tons of plums for the conserve manufacturers – Scott of Carluke, Robertson of Paisley and Smedley of Dundee and Coupar Angus.

The village of Dalserf photographed from the west, close to the banks of the Clyde. The church is on the left and Dalserf House is in the centre.

This is a very early photograph of Dalserf, a view of the village from the west, probably in the 1890s. The main village thoroughfare seen here is not named in the 1891 census, but was later known as Kirk Road. At this time the houses to the right were occupied by John and Janet Ritchie and their daughters, Margaret and Mary. Next door was son Lawrence, his wife Mary and his then family of four.

Five year old Janet Clark Ritchie, sitting in the grass by the gate to Dalserf House, photographed by Charles Reid of Wishaw around 1904. Reid later sold the image to a postcard publisher. The daughter of Lawrence Ritchie and Mary Hamilton McDonald (married 1885), Janet was born at Dalserf on 14th March 1899 and spent her early working life in domestic service before working at an aircraft factory at Clydebank during the First World War. In April 1928 she married 29 year old John Murray, an engineer from Waterloo, at Dalserf Manse and remained in the village until 1988 when she became the first resident in Ballantine Nursing Home, Ashgill. She died there on 4th January 2007 aged 107 years.

Janet Ritchie is the little girl on the right of the two girls opposite the Ritchie house at 1 Kirk Road where the barrel rests. Her brother Lawrence is in charge of the horse and cart while the distant figure behind, is grandfather and gravedigger, John Ritchie. This cart was used for conveyance; the family also owned a low cart for transporting coal from Cornsilloch and Dalserf Station. When the thatch on 1 Kirk Road was replaced with slates in the 1950s, the family built a garage in the garden as temporary accommodation during the year-long renovations.

The south elevation of Dalserf Parish Church with cottage on the left and garden to the right. The modern church building is said to date from 1655, but an eleventh century hogs back stone, found during renovation work, suggests a Norman building, possibly dedicated to St. Machan or St. Serf. Renovations were carried out in 1818 and again in 1895 when, thanks to the munificence of Sir William Hozier of Mauldslie Castle, the heritors' outlay of £80 was made up to £700. Sir William also gifted a new organ and the clock. The 'Chiatri', 'a hindu domed pavilion' bell tower, was added at this time, showing the contemporary influence of Indian architecture.

Winston Churchill is known to have worshipped here on at least one occasion. His wife, Clementine (Hozier) was related to the Newlands (Hoziers) of Mauldslie, who were staunch members and supporters of the church.

John Ritchie (the church officer) with a spade over his shoulder, and Tam Scott, in Dalserf Parish Churchyard around 1905. Born at Kerse Holm, Lesmahagow in 1836, Ritchie was the son of Lawrence, a carting contractor, and Margaret Moffat. In December 1861, whilst living at Rosebank, he married Janet Clark at Dalserf and settled in the village. They had four children; Lawrence (born 1862), Janet (1865), David (1868) and Margaret (1871). He spent his working life as a labourer or contractor on the Dalserf Estate and was beadle for over 40 years. He died of influenza on 19th October 1909. Tam Scott, then in his sixties, was a neighbour of John Ritchie, and worked as a domestic gardener, also on the estate.

Born in 1827 in Ayrshire's Stair Parish, where his father William Rorison, was the minister, the Reverend Dr. William Peebles Rorison, was licensed by Ayr Presbytery in May 1850 and appointed minister to Dalserf parish the following May. In April 1900 he received a Doctor of Divinity degree from his *alma mater* Glasgow University. He died, at the manse, on 11th March 1907, and in the August, Alexander Barclay of Edinburgh was appointed his successor.

Doctor John Rogerson (with the bicycle) outside his home, Dumcrieff House, on the Ashgill to Netherburn road, around 1903, with his daughter Lily and an elderly gentleman. Born at Urr in Kirkcudbrightshire in 1860, he was living at Lochrutton House, Netherburn when, in August 1894, he married Isabella Jones Wallace of Cambuslang, in the Windsor Hotel in Glasgow's St. Vincent Street. Reverend Rorison of Dalserf officiated. Lily was born in October 1897, when they were living at the house Whinknowe, and died in Glasgow in November 1920 of multiple fractures and septicaemia following an accident – coming down Manse Brae on her bicycle, she was thrown over the handlebars. Her short life had been eventful, driving ambulances in wartime France. A second daughter, Honoria-Isobel Margaret, was born in February 1907. Remembered for his expertise in removing tonsils on his kitchen table, Doctor Rogerson died at Dumcrieff on 6th December 1933, aged 74 years.

Dalserf House was built over a deep mine stretching under the Clyde, which may explain the cracks it developed, leading to its demolition in the 1950s. Built in the 1700s, with a porch and billiard room added in 1894, it consisted of three public rooms, six bedrooms and servants' accommodation set in a sheltered locality surrounded by a lawn. The outside 'offices' comprised of a four stall stable and coach house with garden, vinery and greenhouse. When offered for rent in 1870 it was served by the post runner, who called every day. Dalserf Estate remains in the hands of the long-term owners, the Henderson-Hamilton family.

The Caledonian Railway's Dalserf Railway Station in the early twentieth century, looking south, towards Cornsilloch Colliery. Opened on 1st December 1866 as Ayr Road Station (changed to Dalserf Railway Station on 1st July 1903), it stood on the Coalburn branch and was as important for its freight (mainly coal) as its passenger traffic. It closed in January 1941 but re-opened in May 1945, before closing finally on 1st October 1951. The colliery was owned by Archibald Russell of Hamilton, employing 350 underground and 69 above ground workers.

# Garrion Bridge

On 14th May 1811, the Royal Assent was given to 'An Act for erecting and maintaining a Bridge over the river *Clyde*, near *Garion* and *Dalserf*, in the County of *Lanark*', financed by trustee's subscriptions, amounting to £2,307. 12s. and loans totalling £3,000. The trustees would also be responsible for building and maintaining a 40 feet wide approach road from both the north and south for 100 yards. The bridge opened on 12th January 1818. Appearing before 'The Commissioners for Inquiring into Matters Relating to Public Roads in Scotland' in 1859, John Gibb, clerk and treasurer to the Garion Bridge Trust, reported that £1,250 of the loans had been paid off and that 5% interest was being paid on the remainder. The collection of the pontage (tolls) was let and the average annual income for the previous five years had been £187. The revenue, Mr Gibb said, was falling, due to traffic being diverted onto the Lesmahagow Railway. By 1880 the pontage was let at £121 per annum, although pedestrians crossed free of charge. Originally tolls ranged from six shillings for a six horse coach, chariot, or hearse to one penny for a foot passenger. This photograph also shows Motherwell Town Council's pump house, built in 1918, to take water from the river to their reservoir at Thornhill.

The view north across the bridge to Mill House, with a single motor car, demonstrates the difficulties, as traffic increased in the twentieth century. In January 2002 a single span reinforced concrete bridge, upstream of this one, was opened, creating Garrion Interchange. 11,800 vehicles now cross into North Lanarkshire each working day.

*Above*: A horse-drawn wagon of the 'Springwells Bottling Stores', High Blantyre, drives off along the Lanark road, around 1904 past the Garrion Bridge toll house. The wagon is loaded with Springwells ginger beer in swivel stopper bottles. The initials 'TJ', inscribed under the wagon, shows it to be the work of the Motherwell photographer Thomas Johnstone, then working from Melville Drive.

Alexander Muirhead and his wife Agnes who had married at Overton Farm on 11th June 1875, stand either side of the tollhouse doorway in the early 1900s. He appears in the 1901 Census as a colliery carter, whilst Agnes ran the shop, selling sweets and tobacco. They later moved to the North Lodge at Mauldslie Castle where Alexander was employed as a short grass cutter.

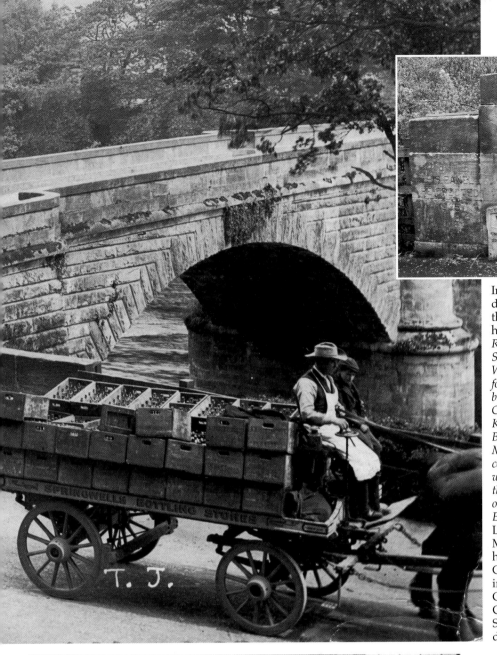

In 1985 the stone plaque from the demolished tollhouse was set into the bridge parapet where the house had stood, and reads; *In testimony of Respect and Gratitude To Sir James Stewart Denham of Coltness and Westshield Bar In whose Patriotic zeal for the improvement of his Country this bridge originated: And by whose liberal Contributions united with those of Mrs Katherine Birnie Mitchelson of Broomhill and The Rev John Scott, DD, Minister of Avendale. It was happily completed in the year 1817. At a time when there was no safe passage across the Clyde from Lanark to Bothwell. The other Contributors erected this tablet. Erected by Ken. Mathieson of Glasgow.* Little is known of Kenneth Mathieson. He was a builder when he married Margaret Anderson at Glasgow in 1807. His other works included Hutcheson's Hall in Glasgow (1802-1805), the White Cart Bridge at Inchinnan (1811), and Stranraer Castle (1820-1822). He died at East Sheen, Surrey in 1859.

The Muirhead family, photographed in the Hamilton Photographic Company's studio at 11 Townhead Street, around 1905. In the centre is Alexander Muirhead, with his wife Agnes to the right, and their son Alex behind. Born in 1885, he later married Jane Ireland Brown and was living in Motherwell's Etna Street, when he died in August 1954. Standing behind, to the left, is Thomas Callan Gray whom the Muirheads adopted following the death of his mother, Jane Gray nee Callan, at his birth in 1879. His wife, from March 1908, Mary Weir Brown is seated front left.

'The Old Tramcar' under the embankment at the south end of Garrion Bridge in its first summer at this location, 1906. It had been a horse-drawn tram, built at the Edinburgh Street Tramway Company's coachworks at Shrubhill, the design winning them a gold medal at the Edinburgh Exhibition of 1886. Their assets were split in 1894, with 70 of their fleet of 100 trams going to the newly-formed Edinburgh District Tramways Company and 30 retained on the Leith and Portobello lines. The service was taken over by Leith Corporation, who electrified the traction, and sold the horses and trams. The 'Street Tramways Company' badge can be seen on the side, below the centre window.

Garrion Mill from the south bank, above Garrion Bridge, with the road to Dalserf running to the right. There is said to have been a mill here from medieval times but references to it may refer to the 'old mill' a few hundred yards upstream on the south bank. This mill, however, was owned by Archibald Brownlie from the late eighteenth century, and passed to his descendants.

Garrion Mill in its latter days, with its 'For man beast fowl, better canna be' advertising slogan. In the spring of 1907 the Brownlie family sold the business to James McGregor, who also owned The Town Mill, Strathaven, Milton Mill at Lesmahagow, and Carmichael Mill at Thankerton. Driven by a lade, it had seven pairs of millstones and a barley stone, with cleaning and finishing machinery for corn bruising, cake nutting, and hay chopping. As part of a modernisation programme, McGregor installed high speed steel grinders, new maize and wheat cutters, and separators and mixers. In March 1970 the mill was extensively damaged by a fire, thought to have been started by boys sheltering during a fishing expedition on a wet Sunday afternoon. On the Tuesday following the Town Mill at Strathaven was also damaged by fire.

Jacob's Ladder, the stepped pathway down the west side of Garrion Gill from Overton, past Castlehill, to the footbridge over Garrion Burn. It would have served as a path from Overton to the Garriongill collieries to the east, but it is not known who cut the steps and added the handrail – mine owners were not quite that safety conscious. However, when the railways opened up the countryside, it was a popular destination for those arriving at Benthead Station on an outing.

Alexander McVake, his wife Ann nee Dempster with their son Robert, photographed in the early 1890s, when living at 'The Glen' near Blair Farm. Both were born in 1838, he at Dillarburn and she at Colinton in Edinburgh, and married at Lesmahagow in November 1857. Robert was the last of their six children, born in 1878. A miner all his working life, he died in April 1899 at Cornsilloch, whilst she survived until 86 years old in 1924.

2330.C.R.

# Garrion

*Left*: Gathering in the harvest of corn on Garrion Farm about a hundred years ago, from a field facing south over the Clyde. It has not been possible to name the couple – or the dog – in the photograph, but the management of the farm was at that time still in the hands of John Warnock (1825-1908) and worked by his sons James and John. However, James Hamilton Warnock, the son of James and Mary Hamilton, born in 1893, was the future of the 70 acre farm.

*Opposite lower*: Garrion Farm around the same period. The hay is being brought in by workers hired for the task. It was a mixed farm with 30 milk cows, hay, grain, fruit and vegetables. The fruit ranged through strawberries, raspberries, red currants, black currants, rhubarb and plums, whilst the vegetables included cabbages, cauliflowers, parsley, leeks and tomatoes. Harvesting this part of the farm's produce needed up to 80 workers. Living on the farm at this time, in addition to the immediate family, were John Jackson (a nephew of John, senior) in his fifties, as ploughman, and local girl Jessie Shaw, a dairymaid, in her twenties.

*Below*: Workers on Garrion making their way up the rows of cauliflower, cultivating and weeding with their hoes. In the spring of 1949, James Warnock was host to a German manufacturer's demonstration of horticultural machines, one of which carried out the task being performed by these men.

With the river forming a natural defence on three sides, Garrion Tower was a typical, three storey, sixteenth century fortified tower and was the summer residence of the Bishop of Glasgow and Galloway. Its size was trebled with two nineteenth century additions. James Warnock of Garrion Farm bought it in 1939.

Part of Garrion Farm's 40 head of cattle in the field below Garrion Tower, around 1904.

# Castlehill Farm

David Gibson Wingate of Castlehill Farm, Cambusnethan, with his wife Jessie, sowing corn in the spring of 1903. He inherited the 100 acre farm from his father, Andrew Wingate who, at his death in April 1898, was described as a farmer at Castlehill and a baker in Wishaw. David employed his elder brother John as a ploughman. In 1899 he married 28 year old Jessie Martin of Wemysshill Orchard, who had been housekeeper to her widowed father Robert Martin. They had a son Andrew, born in 1900.

With the hopper filled, David strides out across the field broadcasting the seed.

With children and horses at the gate to the farm.

# Wemysshill Farm

Thomas Paterson (centre) of Wemysshill Farm, Cambusnethan, with his ploughman Stewart Smith and his hind (farm servant) Andrew Allison, harrowing one of his fields looking to Overton Colliery around 1903. The family had been on the 130 acre farm since the early nineteenth century. Thomas, born in January 1855, succeeded his father, Robert Paterson, and himself was succeeded by his son John, born in 1895. His obituary in the *Scotsman*, in December 1933, speaks of how well-known he was throughout south west Scotland as a breeder of farm stock and Clydesdale horses.

Workers at Wemysshill having a break for tea whilst building stacks. The horse on the left is working a sledge, to collect the sheaves, whilst the one to the right is harnessed to a rake.

Thrashing oats at Wemysshill Farm. The oats would have been cut, and bound into sheaves, in late August or early September and left to stand for three weeks before being made into stacks. Over winter, the hired thrashing machine would make half a dozen visits, processing five or six stacks each time. Twelve men were needed and farms worked communally, helping each other, as the thrasher made its way round. Two hundredweights of seed produced two tons of grain, used at Wemysshill as cattle feed over winter.

# Cambusnethan House

Now a roofless ruin, the Scottish Baronial style Cambusnethan Priory was designed by the Dunblane born architect James Gillespie Graham in 1819-1820, for Sir Robert Sinclair-Lockhart of Castlehill. The previous house had been a summer residence for the Bishops of Glasgow, hence the appellation 'Priory', but was lost to a fire in 1816. The family line on the estate, in Scotland, ended with the death of Sir Graeme Alexander Sinclair-Lockhart in 1904, his successor having emigrated to New Zealand. There was a succession of tenants until it sold for conversion to an hotel and 'medieval banqueting hall' in 1973 which ended with a major fire in 1985.

Sir Graeme Alexander Sinclair-Lockhart shortly before his death in March 1904, at the age of 84 years, with his wife Emilia Udny Brebner who died the following June. Choosing a military career, he joined the 78th Highlanders, the Ross-shire Buffs, as a 17 year old, in 1837 and was posted to India in 1842. He took part in the Persian War of 1856 and the Indian Mutiny in 1857, as a captain, and was mentioned in dispatches at the Battle of Lucknow. By 1867, as major-general, he commanded the regiment. On retiring from the army, the couple returned to Cambusnethan and were active in promoting the welfare of the community in and around the estate. They were laid to rest in a mausoleum within the grounds of the house. His medals are held in the Buffs Museum at Fort George, near Inverness.

A carte de visite featuring Cambusnethan House, produced by the Wishaw photographer Charles Reid. Cartes de visite generally carried the photograph of an individual or family and became popular in the 1860s, when they replaced their predecessors, the much more expensive tintypes and daguerrotypes. The name derives from their being the same size as contemporary visiting cards. This one has been endorsed, and would have been presented, by Sir Graeme Duncan Power Sinclair-Lockhart, over an array of Reid's associateships. Sir Graeme was the 12th baronet of Murkle (Caithness) and Stevenson (Haddingtonshire) and succeeded to the title in 1918. He was educated in New Zealand and Cambridge University and served as a 2nd Lieutenant with the Scottish Horse in Egypt and Palestine during the First World War, and in the Russo-Finnish War (1939-40). He died in 1959.

*Left*: Seven year old Janet Burnside at one of the Lion Pillars guarding the entrance to Cambusnethan Woods in 1963. Before moving to Netherton, Wishaw, her parents, James and Elizabeth *nee* Twaddle, were employed on the estate, as her grandparents had been also. Her paternal grandmother, Janet Craig Twaddle, had been a servant at Cambusnethan, and her maternal grandfather, Lancelot Twaddle, had farmed at Carbarns Farm before the Second World War. He bred Clydesdale horses and after years of entering classes at the Royal Highland Show won, posthumously, the 'Best of Breed' class in 1962.

# Dalziel House

Dalzell House is a fifteenth century tower house re-modelled in the 1850s, by the architects Brown and Wardrop of Edinburgh, and Robert William Billings of London, for John Glencairn Carter Hamilton, 1st Baron Hamilton of Dalzell. The family had made its fortune on coal under the estate. Following the death of the 80 year old 2nd Earl, Gavin George Hamilton, in 1952, part of the house became Gresham School. Motherwell and Wishaw Town Council bought it in 1967. Many years on the house was sold and developed into apartments.

The Japanese Garden at Dalzell House, was the creation of Lady Sybil Hamilton who married Gavin George Hamilton, 2nd Baron of Dalzell, in July 1912. On the banks of the Dalzell Burn, its pond, azaleas and rhododendrons, created settings for the many ornamental statues. This flight of steps was modelled on the temple at Nagasaki. Little of it survives except the bamboo and the maples.

As with country houses across the country, Dalzell House was a hospital for wounded soldiers during the First World War, supervised by Lady Hamilton, whilst Lord Hamilton was at the front with his regiment, the Scots Guards. The first batch, comprising of ten Belgian and six British soldiers, wounded at the front line, arrived in November 1914. Within a few months the Motherwell branch of the Soldiers' and Sailors' Association were inviting them to entertainment evenings in the town hall. This later group, were photographed in the grounds of the House having been presented with baskets of strawberries.

*Above and opposite*: Part of the architect Robert W Billings' task was to ensure that his work on the house was reflected in the garden, hence this classic parterre, or sunken garden. It would have been the work of the head gardener, William Cassels, who used box hedge for the lines and alpines and annuals for the beds. Born in 1793, Cassels followed his father James into this occupation and spent his working life at Dalzell. In 1812 he married Mary Jamieson and one of their children, Andrew, has at times been credited with the work at Dalzell, despite having been a grocer. William died on Christmas Day 1877, aged 84 years, at Gateside Street, Hamilton.

Hudson & Kearns

# Ross House

Built around a core dating from 1783, Ross House was designed by the architect Alexander Cullen of Quarry Street, Hamilton in 1888 on a commission from Thomas Stokes George Hugh Robertson-Aikman. The following contractors were involved in the work: masonry, Messrs Brown and Henderson of Hamilton; joinery, Messrs William Chambers & Co. of Motherwell; plumbing, Messrs Brown & Young of Glasgow; roofing and plastering, William McGhie of Hamilton.

Born at New Parks in Leicestershire on 25th February 1860, Colonel Thomas Stokes George Hugh Robertson-Aikman of Ross and Broomhilton in Lanarkshire, and Grandborough in Warwickshire, was the eldest son of Hugh Henry Robertson-Aikman. Educated at Eton and Brasenose College, Oxford, he married Constance Henrietta Middleton of Kilmaron Castle, Fife on 29th April 1899. An enthusiastic sportsman, he played cricket for Eton and captained Oxford, later turning his interests to curling and foxhunting. In 1884 he was elected president (for life) of Hamilton and Thornyhill Curling Club, and in 1924 captained the British curling team to Gold at the Chamonix Winter Olympics. He rode with the Lanarkshire and Renfrewshire Foxhounds and was master of the hunt between 1896 and 1901. In 1880 he joined the Royal Lanarkshire Militia (later, 4th Battalion, Highland Light Infantry) and was appointed its commanding officer in 1900. He died at The Ross on 18th April 1948. The family name is remembered in Aikman Road in Motherwell and Aikman Green, Grandborough in Warwickshire.

The bridge carrying the driveway to Ross House over the Avon Water from the Motherwell to Hamilton road, around 1908. It is not known when it, or the gatehouse, was built, but a bridge appears at this spot on John Thomson's, 1832, Map of Scotland.

Colonel T S G H Robertson-Aikman (third from the left) with the Lanarkshire and Renfrewshire Foxhounds in the winter of 1896. Founded in 1771, they met every Tuesday and Saturday morning at farms and estates throughout the two counties over winter.

Construction of the Lanarkshire Tramways Company's three mile and three furlong line from Cadzow Street, Hamilton to London Street, Larkhall, along Carlisle Road, passing the south entrance to Ross Estate in the spring of 1905. On 15th July the first trams from Hamilton ran as far as Ferniegair Station, and the following week to Larkhall. The full journey fare was 3d.

# The River Avon.

The River Avon, looking up stream from its confluence with the Clyde, to the bridge at the entrance to Ross House, and the estate on the left. On the right a tramcar makes its way from Motherwell to Hamilton under the shadow of Langloan Strip Wood. The angler's task of hooking a trout or grayling, would not have been helped by the boys in the water.

The pictures below left and right are sections taken from the main photograph.

# Hamilton Palace

The north front of Hamilton Palace in the spring of 1906. Once a thirteenth century tower house, work on the 'grandest seat in Scotland', began in 1695 when William, 3rd Duke of Hamilton commissioned the architect James Smith to design and erect the south front – a century and a half would elapse before the work was completed. In the 1730s the architect William Adam was commissioned by the 5th Duke to redesign and build the north front (265 feet long and 60 feet high), but many years, and the duke, would pass away before its completion. William Adam too would be long gone, and the architect David Hamilton finally saw it finished in 1842, for the 10th Duke.

The south front, and the formal entrance to the palace, with its pedimented, four column portico.

The morning room at the palace, photographed by James Lafayette (1853-1923) before the contents came under the auctioneer's hammer in 1919. Born in Dublin, early fame offered work in London, including the jubilee photographs of Queen Victoria. This photograph, however, does not fully represent the extensive collection of *objects d'art* brought to the palace by the 10th Duke, Alexander Douglas-Hamilton (1767-1852), an avid art collector. The first of the 'family silver' sales was in London in June 1882, which included paintings by Titian, Tintoretto and Botticelli, a number of which were bought by the National Gallery in London.

When the 12tth Duke, William Alexander Louis Stephen, died in 1895, at the age of 50 years, he left explicit instructions for the disposal of his estate, once his debts had been settled. He had only one child, Lady Mary Louise Hamilton, who succeeded to the Arran and Easton estates. The trustees, with regard to Hamilton Palace, were given the power; 'to entirely displenish and dismantle it, and take down and remove the building or allow the same to fall into disuse'. This photograph shows one lot at the sale of the furniture and fittings, held there in November 1919, consisting of one settee (nine feet six inches long), one small settee (six feet long), four armchairs and six small chairs, all in English gilt with silk flowered brocade.

With work on the palace complete, Alexander, 10th Duke of Hamilton, commissioned the Edinburgh based architect David Bryce to design the Mausoleum, with its chapel and vaults. The work was three years from completion when the 85 year old Duke died in 1852. Standing 120 feet high, on a 110 feet diameter base, it had three levels: a basement, a superstructure and an 18 feet dome, and a final cost of £130,000.

An early 1920s group of visitors photographed outside the Mausoleum demonstrates the continued interest in the edifice.

The catacombs held the remains of sixteen members of the family, from The Most High and Puissant Prince John, 1st Marquis of Hamilton and 3rd Duke of Chatelherault, who died at Hamilton on 12th April 1604, to Alexander, 10th Duke of Hamilton, Brandon and Chatelherault, who had commissioned the mausoleum. Early in 1852 the bodies of family members past were brought from the old church of Hamilton to rest here. The recumbent lions, each sculpted from a single piece of freestone, were by the Edinburgh sculptor Alexander Handyside Ritchie, who also carved the three masks, representing Life, Death and Immortality, over the entrance. The stone came from quarries in the Glasgow area, some owned by the family.

The lion to the left of the entrance of the mausoleum being cleaned around 1903. Their guard duty would be over in 1921 when mine workings threatened the whole edifice with collapse. In the event it only sank some 18 inches. In May that year, a petition was granted at Hamilton Sheriff Court to remove the remains of past dukes and re-inter them at Hamilton's Bent Cemetery. Wyllie and Lochhead of Glasgow was tasked with the work of removing and re-burying the sixteen cadavers and four small chests containing hearts.

Designed as a summer house and hunting lodge, by the architect, mason and entrepreneur William Adam in 1730, Chatelherault takes its name from the French dukedom of Chatelherault, conferred on the Hamilton family in 1550. Building work ran from 1732 until 1744 and, although some saw it as a folly, it served as stables, dog kennels, a hunting lodge and banqueting rooms.

They are thought to be descended from the Auroch, an early breed of European ox. The white cattle, seen here amongst the oaks of Cadzow Forest in the late nineteenth century, have the distinctive markings of white coats with black muzzles, ears and feet. When brought to Britain, possibly by the Romans, they had a religious significance, which Christianity displaced and the cattle were then put into the wild for hunting. Today there are two herds, one at Strathclyde Park and the other at Chillingham in Northumberland. In the late 1960s the survivors of this herd were moved to East Lothian, but in 1987 a small group was returned to the newly opened Chatelherault Country Park.

# Clyde Bridge

The Clyde Bridge, or Hamilton Bridge as it was originally known, carried the road over the Clyde between Motherwell and Hamilton from 1780 when it was built by Hamilton Town Council to a design by James Watt. John Smeaton is credited with a joint design but his fee of £10.10s. was too high compared to Watt's at £7.7s. and he was not engaged. Building work took nine years from 1771, but in September 1807 a flood carried away one of the central piers and two arches, and a temporary wooden bridge was in place until 1827 when re-building was completed.

As early as 1872 it was proposed to build a tramway system from Glasgow to Bothwell and Hamilton, with a branch line to Motherwell and Wishaw, but nothing came of it. In 1899, thanks to Hamilton Town Council, the Hamilton, Motherwell and Wishaw Tramways Company was formed, and on 27th July 1903 the line opened, operating under the name Lanarkshire Tramways Company. It was an instant success – the system carrying 106,500 passengers over the 1904 New Year holiday. Its continued success, and profitability, seemed assured until competition from buses forced closure on St Valentine's Day 1931.

In August 1926 the Ministry of Transport approved the building of the new Clyde Bridge. The Motherwell Bridge and Engineering Company, in conjunction with Messrs Melville Dundas & Whitson of Glasgow, won the contract. The £82,000 venture was the combined enterprise of Lanarkshire County Council with the burghs of Hamilton, Motherwell and Wishaw. The 400 feet long and three span structure of steel and concrete, would have an 80 feet wide carriageway and 10 feet wide footpaths on either side and be competed in two years. However, it did not open until December 1931 when it did so without formal ceremony.

Clyde Bridge, looking to Motherwell with the Coronation Arch, erected in 1953 to celebrate the coronation of Queen Elizabeth II. It was brought from London and gifted to Motherwell and Wishaw Council by Thomas R Miller of Motherwell Bridge and Engineering Company, and was in place until 1969 when corrosion forced its removal.

# Bothwell Bridge

A late nineteenth century view of the four span Bothwell Bridge from the south bank, showing how easy access to the river bank once was. The earliest surviving record of the bridge dates to 1647, when the government contributed to its repair. From 1787 it carried the Glasgow to Carlisle mail coach. In the 1790s the Rev Michael MacCulloch wrote of its 'old and narrow scale' and that there was a proposal to have it rebuilt on a larger scale. This, however, was not undertaken until 1826 when the carriageway was widened from 12 to 32 feet. The cast iron walkways were added to the outside of each parapet in 1871. With work nearing completion, 15 year old apprentice painter Andrew Greig fell from the scaffolding on 27th December and drowned, his body being found the following April at Glasgow. The house on the left was in the grounds of Fairleigh House on Bothwell Road.

The view north across the bridge around 1910 to Bridge House, occupied by Peter Ross, gardener to Fairleigh House which stands behind, and was home to the Coalmaster James Stedman Dixon. Having passed the monument and coming on to the bridge is a Lanarkshire Tramways Company's tram from Uddingston, bound for Hamilton. Work on the route had started in March 1908.

The public park, or 'lido', adjoining the bridge was developed in 1935-36 with the assistance of a government grant of £5,200 towards the full cost of £7,500, under the terms of the Special Areas (Development and Improvement) Act of 1935. The cost included, not only the laying out of the park and a children's play area, but the building of the embankment wall. The wall survives, but the floral beds have since given way to (less labour-intensive to maintain) trees.

From 1896 the National Convention of Reformed Churches held an annual service here to commemorate the Battle of Bothwell Bridge on 20th June 1679. Out of this evolved the National Memorial Committee, under the Duke of Hamilton, formed to raise the funding to erect a suitable monument. With over £750 raised, the monumental sculptor, Scott and Rae of Glasgow's Eglinton Street was commissioned. Using granite from Rubislaw Quarry near Aberdeen, they fashioned the 40 feet high obelisk on its 100 square feet base, and with bronze plates – *'Blessed are they which are persecuted for righteousness sake', 'Be thou faithful unto death and I will give thee a crown of life'* and *'The righteous shall be in everlasting remembrance'*. It was unveiled by Lord Overtoun at a ceremony on 20th June 1903 before a crowd of 15,000.

# Strathclyde Park

The view south across the pond in Clyde Park, in the 1920s when, despite the pier, recreational facilities went little beyond pike fishing. To the north, over the photographer's shoulder, the village of Bothwellhaugh was still flourishing. Forty years and more would pass before the mine and its village were deserted and the pond enlarged to Strathclyde Loch.

Similar view across the water but now, having realised the potential for income, Motherwell and Wishaw Council have upgraded the pier and brought in a fleet of rowing boats.

View of the Roman Bridge with the later footbridge visible through the arch.

The footbridge over South Calder Water, upstream from Roman Bridge, built around 1908.

# Bothwellhaugh

Hamilton Palace Colliery 'The Pailice' in the early 1920s when it was at the peak of its productive life, employing a workforce of 1,480 – 1,200 underground and 280 surface workers – producing 2,000 tons of coal per day. Opened in 1884, on 800 acres of ground leased from the Duke of Hamilton, the Bent Colliery Company came upon a rich seam of splint coal, the coal of choice for railway steam locomotive operators. Eventually two shafts, each reaching a depth of 950 feet, were in operation. When it was taken over by the National Coal Board in 1947 it had no baths, no canteen and no medical facilities, and closed in 1959.

The members of the Mining Institute of Scotland on a visit to the 'Pailice' in August 1899, when they were received by the managing director, Mr. James S Dixon (1850-1911). The 'Pailice' was at the forefront of mining technology and there would have been much to learn. Despite many mining fatalities over the years, the Institute's genesis was a firedamp explosion at Blantyre in 1877, killing two men. This highlighted the issue of safety and, coupled with the struggle to increase efficiency through pooled knowledge, led to the founding of the West of Scotland Mining Institute, later becoming the national body.

Girl sorters, whose job was to pick stone and debris from the coal as it passed along a conveyor belt, photographed around 1925. Long past were the days when women carried coal-filled creels to the surface for their menfolk, but even picking was not without its dangers, a number of them falling into machinery adjacent to the conveyor belt.

A 1910 investigation into housing for miners in Lanarkshire, by the county medical officer, found that of the 1205 employees in Bothwellhaugh, 965 lived in mine owners' houses, of which there were 450. There were two churches, two schoolhouses, a co-operative system general store and a recreation hall, but no public house. Annual rents ranged from the basic single apartment at £4.17s 6d to the three apartment house, with scullery, water closet and bath, at £15.12s. with the company paying the rates. The houses were good standard, with damp-proof courses and ventilation. Following the closure of the pit in 1959, families drifted away through the early 1960s, leaving the housing to demolition in 1966, when this photograph was taken. Much of the site of the village now lies under the loch in Strathclyde Park.